Take a trip to
WALES

Keith Lye
General Editor
Henry Pluckrose

Franklin Watts

London   New York   Sydney   Toronto

Facts about Wales

Area:
20,761 sq. km.
(8,016 sq. miles)

Population:
2,792,000

Capital:
Cardiff

Largest cities:
Cardiff (279,800)
Swansea (187,900)
Newport (130,200)

Official languages:
English, Welsh

Religion:
Christianity

Main products:
Coal, metals and metal
products; cattle, dairy
products, sheep and wool;
cereals and vegetables

Currency:
Pound

Franklin Watts Limited
12a Golden Square
London W1

ISBN: UK Edition 0 86 313 441 6
ISBN: US Edition 0 531 10197 5
Library of Congress Catalog
Card No: 86 50020

© Franklin Watts Limited 1986

Typeset by Ace Filmsetting Ltd,
Frome, Somerset
Printed in Hong Kong

Maps: Tony Payne

Design: Edward Kinsey

Stamps: Stanley Gibbons Limited

Photographs: Chris Fairclough, 10;
Zefa, 4, 17, 18, 22, 23; Robert Harding,
3, 13, 20; J. Allan Cash, 8, 12, 14, 19, 21,
24, 25, 26; Britain on View, 5, 6, 7, 9, 15,
16, 27, 29, 30; Welsh National Opera, 31
Front cover: Zefa
Back cover: Chris Fairclough

Wales is the smallest of the three
countries which make up Great
Britain. The others are England and
Scotland. Mountains cover about
two-thirds of Wales. The tallest
mountain, Snowdon, is 1,085 m
(3,560 ft) above sea level. Coastal
plains and fertile valleys make up
most of the rest of Wales.

Wales has two official languages: English and Welsh. About 19 out of every 100 people speak Welsh, a Celtic language which resembles Breton, which is spoken in Brittany, France. The Welsh name for the country is Cymru.

The Welsh are proud of their ancient traditions. They hold festivals, called eisteddfodau, of music, poetry and drama. The picture shows dancers at the International Eisteddfod which is held at Llangollen, in North Wales.

The Celts invaded Wales about 2,600 years ago. The Romans ruled Wales from the AD 60s until the early fifth century, when Wales became independent. England's Saxon rulers built an earth bank shown here and trench along the Welsh border to stop attacks by Welsh raiders. It was called Offa's Dyke.

Saint David (Dewi in Welsh) is the country's patron saint. Saint David lived in the sixth century. His home was a village in southwestern Wales, which is now called St David's. It contains St David's Cathedral. Most people in Wales are Protestants. The Methodists form the largest group.

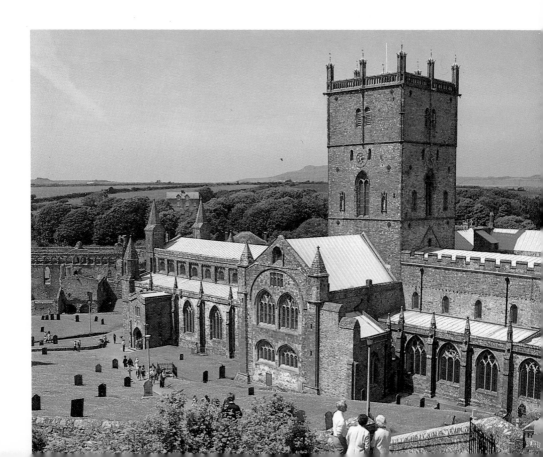

Wales came under English rule in 1282. King Edward I gave his son, who became Edward II, the title of Prince of Wales. Wales remains a principality. In 1969, Queen Elizabeth II gave her son, Charles, this ancient title at a ceremony in Caernarfon Castle.

Pembroke Castle in southwestern Wales was the birthplace of a Welsh prince, Henry Tudor, who became King Henry VII in 1485. He was the first Welsh King of England. In 1536, his son, Henry VIII, united England and Wales under a single government.

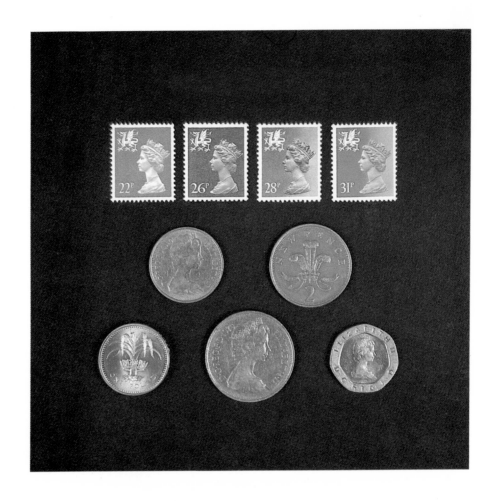

The picture shows some stamps and money used in Wales. The notes and coins used in Wales are the same as those used in the rest of Great Britain.

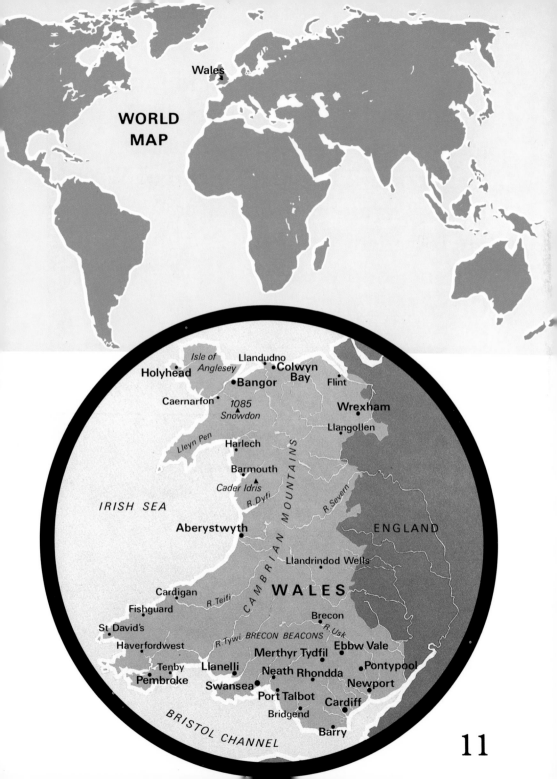

WORLD MAP

Wales

Isle of Anglesey
Llandudno
Holyhead
Colwyn Bay
Bangor
Flint
Caernarfon
1085 Snowdon
Wrexham
Llangollen
Lleyn Pen
Harlech
Barmouth
Cader Idris
R. Dyfi
IRISH SEA
R. Severn
ENGLAND
Aberystwyth
Llandrindod Wells
CAMBRIAN MOUNTAINS
WALES
Cardigan
R. Teifi
Fishguard
Brecon
R. Usk
St David's
BRECON BEACONS
Ebbw Vale
Haverfordwest
R. Tywi
Merthyr Tydfil
Pontypool
Tenby
Llanelli
Neath
Rhondda
Newport
Pembroke
Swansea
Port Talbot
Cardiff
Bridgend
Barry
BRISTOL CHANNEL

11

Cardiff is the capital and largest city of Wales. Wales elects 38 members to the British House of Commons. The chief official of Wales is the Secretary of State for Wales. He is a member of the British Cabinet and he heads the Welsh Office in Cardiff.

Swansea in South Wales is the
second largest city. It is a major
seaport with many industries. The
picture shows an oil refinery. Swansea
(called Abertawe in Welsh) is in West
Glamorgan, one of the eight counties
of Wales.

Newport is the third largest city in Wales. Its docks are on the estuary of the River Usk. It is an industrial city, with the remains of a Norman castle. Caerleon, near Newport, is the site of an old Roman fortress.

The Menai Bridge connects mainland Wales to the largest island, Anglesey. The Welsh call Anglesey Môn Mam Cymru, which means Mon, Mother of Wales, because it once produced most of the grain for North Wales.

Wales has much magnificent
coastal scenery and golden beaches.
The Gower peninsula which juts out
into the Bristol Channel in South
Wales near Swansea, has some of the
country's most beautiful bays and
coves.

16

Tenby is a major resort in South Wales. The southwestern coasts of Wales form a national park. Wales also contains Snowdonia National Park in the north and the Brecon Beacons National Park in the southeast.

About a third of Welsh workers are employed in industry. Wales produces 7.5 percent of Britain's coal. But coal mining is declining because of falling demand. This mine is in the Rhondda valley in South Wales.

Limestone and slate are also mined. Limestone is used for building, in road works and for the production of lime, which has many uses in industry. Slate comes mostly from North Wales. It is used for roofing houses.

Wales has many metal industries. The picture shows a steelworks in South Wales. Wales once produced much iron ore, but most of it is now imported from Spain. Steel and tinplate are both important products.

In recent years, many new industries, including chemicals, electronics and plastics, have started up in Wales. These industries are replacing older, declining ones. The picture shows a chipboard factory in northeast Wales.

Farmland covers four-fifths of Wales. Most crops, including barley, oats, potatoes and other vegetables, are grown on the lowlands, where the climate is mild. Dairy farming is also important on the lowlands.

The uplands of Wales are cooler and much wetter than the lowlands. Beef cattle are reared in hill country, where there is plenty of rich pasture. Sheep are well suited to regions with steep slopes.

Wales has the same school system as England and education is compulsory and free for children between 5 and 16. The picture shows a music class in a school in Cardiff.

The Welsh language is taught in schools and school libraries contain books in both English and Welsh. Welsh language is transmitted on two television channels.

Wales has one university, consisting of colleges in Aberystwyth (shown here), Bangor, Cardiff and Swansea. It also includes the College of Medicine and the Institute of Science and Technology, both in Cardiff, and St David's College in Lampeter.

Rugby football is the leading sport in Wales. Welsh rugby supporters travel long distances to see Wales compete in an annual international rugby championship with England, France, Ireland and Scotland. Soccer and cricket are also played in Wales.

Boating, walking and climbing are popular outdoor activities. This picture shows Lake Bala, the country's largest natural lake, in North Wales. Its Welsh name is Llyn Tegid.

The Brecon Beacons National Park contains mountains, rising to 886 m (2,907 ft), lakes, waterfalls and moorland. It is excellent walking country for family outings.

Wales has been a land of poets for more than 1,000 years. A great Welsh poem, written in about AD 600, is the Gododdin. It describes a battle in Yorkshire. The best known modern Welsh poet, Dylan Thomas, wrote poetry in this hut at Laugharne, in South Wales.

Wales is also a land of music and song. The Welsh National Opera was set up in 1946 and it now enjoys a great reputation for its productions. Here the company is performing "The Cunning Little Vixen", an opera by the Czech composer Leos Janacek.

Index